Coast

T0045462

Where on Earth?

THE GREAT LAKES

We know quite a lot about the Great Lakes thanks to photos taken from space. Thousands of satellite photos, such as this one, help scientists study each lake and how it changes over time. Slow-moving glaciers carved out valleys and made deep, hollowed-out areas on Earth between 1.6 million and 10,000 years ago. Later, when the area got warmer, the melting water filled the hollow areas and formed the lakes. Each lake has a distinct shape, but there are other differences, too. The lakes are different sizes, and a variety of landscapes surround them. Read more about each lake here.

> If the lakes look funny to you in this image, remember that a satellite can take a photo from many different angles. In this satellite photo, Lake Superior is at the bottom rather than on the left, where it appears on a map. But if you turn a map of the Great Lakes on its side so that Lake Superior is at the bottom, you'll be able to tell how the satellite was turned when it took this photo from space.

Lake Huron

Average Depth: 195 ft.

Lake Huron has 30,000 islands. One is the world's largest freshwater island, which has a lake on it—and that lake has an island in it!

It is second largest by area, about the size of West Virginia.

A drop of water stays in Lake Huron for 22 years. That is how long it takes the lake to refill with all new water.

< Fishermen know that the burbot is a good fish for eating. Burbot live in all five of the Great Lakes.

Lake Superior

Average Depth: 483 ft.

The Chippewa Indians called Lake Superior *Gitche Gumee* (Big Water). Yes, it's big. It's the biggest Great Lake.

This lake could fill all the other Great Lakes, plus three more Lake Eries. It's the deepest and coldest of the five lakes. It also has the cleanest water.

Lake Superior's water empties slowly into Lake Huron. A drop of water stays in Lake Superior for 191 years.

NATIONAL
GEOGRAPHIC

Ladders

Great LAKES

WHERE ON EARTH?

The Fresh

by *Chris Siegel*

So, where are the Great Lakes, and what makes them so great? The five Great Lakes are Lake Superior, Lake Michigan, Lake Huron, Lake Erie, and Lake Ontario. These lakes are so huge that if you stood on one side of any of them, you would not be able to see across the lake to the land on the opposite shore. The Great Lakes are located in the United States and Canada, in the center of North America. This area is called the Great Lakes basin. A **basin** is an area with sides sloping up, like a shallow bowl, so all the water in the area drains toward the center. The lakes have many **tributaries**, or connecting rivers and streams. Together, the lakes and their tributaries contain the largest supply of fresh water on the planet—that's pretty great!

People have lived along the lakes for thousands of years. They've used the lake water for drinking, fishing, and moving from place to place. In fact, the Great Lakes are really helpful when it comes to moving goods around the world. Even though they are located in the center of North America, a network of rivers and canals connects these lakes to the ocean. This makes it possible for a cargo ship to get from Europe all the way to Chicago, Illinois.

Miners Castle on Michigan's Upper Peninsula is part of Lake Superior's more than 2,700 miles of shoreline.

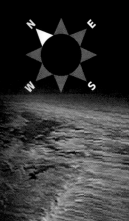

Lake Ontario

Average Depth: 283 ft.

Water from Lake Erie flows over Niagara Falls into Lake Ontario. Then Lake Ontario's water flows into the St. Lawrence River, which flows to the Atlantic Ocean.

Ontario's water is the most polluted because pollution from other lakes drains into it.

A drop of water remains in Lake Ontario for about six years.

Lake Erie

Average Depth: 62 ft.

Compared to the other four lakes, Lake Erie is shallow—it holds the least amount of water of all the Great Lakes.

But Lake Erie is no squirt—it is the 12th-largest lake in the world. And it supplies us with more fish to eat than the other Great Lakes combined.

A drop of water stays in Lake Erie only 2.6 years.

The Dwarf Lake Iris is the official state wildflower of Michigan. This flower grows wild in the Great Lakes region. It does not grow wild anywhere else in the world.

Lake Michigan

Average Depth: 279 ft.

Lake Michigan is the largest freshwater lake entirely within in the United States, and the fifth-largest lake in the world!

Some of Lake Michigan's beaches are covered in "sugar sand," which looks just like sugar.

A drop of water stays in Lake Michigan for 99 years.

Check In   How were the Great Lakes formed?

5

The Lake Effect

by David Holford

A winter storm is brewing over Lake Superior's Upper Peninsula. This area of the country gets lots of lake-effect snow.

Who hasn't been excited to wake up in the morning, look outside, and see the air thick with snowflakes and deep snowdrifts on the ground? School has been cancelled because a "lake-effect" storm has brought 18 inches of snow!

Many people living near the Great Lakes have to deal with the **lake effect**, or the way that a large lake influences weather in places nearby. The most extreme lake effect is snow—and lots of it.

When winter comes, the air around the lakes cools more quickly than the water in the lakes does. As cold air blows over the surface of the lakes, it pulls warmth and moisture from the water, forming clouds. Once this warmed air hits land, it cools again. Then the moisture in the clouds falls as snow.

Because the winds that cross the Great Lakes come from the northwest and Canada, the southern and eastern shores of the lakes get the most snow. These regions of heavy snowfall form what is known as a **snowbelt**.

As Earth gradually becomes warmer, the amount of lake-effect snow will increase. That's because it will take longer for ice to form on the Great Lakes during the winter. Less ice means warmer water, and you know what that brings—more snow. Some places in the snowbelt, such as Syracuse, New York, are getting 50 percent more snow per year than they did 100 years ago.

Ice collects along the Lake Superior shoreline in Ontario, Canada.

Snow Day

Hold a yardstick beside you. Now add seven more inches at the top. That's how much snow fell on Syracuse, New York, during a blizzard in early December 2010. A blizzard is a very strong snowstorm. Tumbling snow pounded the city for four days without letting up. The storm started on Sunday, and before it was finished on Wednesday, more than 43 inches covered the ground. During the worst of the storm, as much as two inches of new snow fell each hour. Dozens of schools closed. Police even closed roads as they responded to many accidents in the city and around it.

The blizzard wasn't the only snowfall in Syracuse that month. More snowstorms followed the blizzard, and by December 21, the official first day of winter, six feet of snow had fallen on this snowbelt city.

Since 1951, Syracuse has averaged about ten feet of snow per year. Lake Erie and Lake Ontario cause this heavy lake-effect snow to fall across the snowbelt in western New York. Most Syracuse residents, however, don't seem to mind their extreme winter weather. In fact, they are used to it. That terrible snowstorm of December 2010 didn't slow the city down for long. Syracuse schools were only closed for two days.

A family pitches in to clear snow from the street after the December 2010 Syracuse snowstorm.

The winter of 2010–2011 was one of the snowiest in Syracuse history. This photo shows snow falling in Clinton Square in downtown Syracuse. In total, Syracuse received nearly 15 feet of snow that winter.

People enjoy cool breezes and sunny skies at Chicago's North Avenue Beach. This popular beach is located on the shore of Lake Michigan.

Cooler by the Lake

The winters might be very snowy in a Great Lakes snowbelt, but the summers make up for all that snow. That's because along with a snowy winter, the lake effect can also create a cool and breezy summer. During the summer months, the water in the Great Lakes doesn't get warm nearly as fast as the air and land in the region. As winds blow across the lakes, the cool water absorbs some of the heat from the air. As these winds hit the shore, they become nature's air conditioner. Communities near the lakes can sometimes be ten degrees cooler on summer days than places farther inland, away from the shore.

The people who live along the lakes enjoy this nice side of the lake effect. Buffalo, New York, for example, at the eastern end of Lake Erie, has never had a day when temperatures topped 100 degrees.

Unfortunately, the summertime lake effect can also be dangerous. At summer's end, as temperatures begin to drop, the lakes become warmer than the air, especially at night. This can cause high winds, heavy rains, and severe thunderstorms. By the end of October, however, the air has cooled enough to produce snow instead of rain. Once again, the lake-effect snow season is ready to start. Winter, spring, summer, or fall, the Great Lakes affect the weather around them all year.

How do the Great Lakes affect the weather in nearby regions?

ALIEN

In Florida's Everglades, huge snakes called Burmese pythons slither across watery landscapes, gobbling up native animals. In London, noisy flocks of ring-necked parakeets raid fruit trees and backyard bird feeders, leaving little food for other birds. In Cuba, a woody weed called *marabu*, which can grow ten feet high, takes over huge areas of farmland, turning them into thorny jungles.

What do the pythons, parakeets, and woody weeds have in common? They are all **invasive species**. These species are alien, or not native, to the **ecosystem** in which they are found. They invade it and can cause harm to the local environment.

Invasive animals compete aggressively with native species for food, space, and other resources. They usually have no natural enemies. That means that they have no **predators**, or animals that hunt

Asian carp are known for their large size. They also have an incredible leaping ability.

INVASION

by Brett Gover

and eat them. Their populations grow quickly. Soon they begin crowding out the life-forms originally living in the area they have invaded.

Some species have been carried from their native ecosystems to new ones. Sometimes this is accidental. For example, a seed is transported from one continent to another in a packing crate on a ship. Other times, people bring species from one place to another on purpose. They do

this hoping that it will help rid a region of a pest or solve other similar problems.

The result has been an explosion of invasive species. In the United States, one of the most feared invaders is the Asian carp. After spreading through the Mississippi River system, this large fish now threatens to enter the Great Lakes. How did this happen? What might happen next? Let's find out.

THE INVASION BEGINS!

Asian carp were brought to the United States from eastern Asia on purpose. In the 1970s, fish farmers and government agencies in the southern United States began importing Asian carp to keep the water in their ponds and lagoons clean. These fish keep water clear by eating microscopic plants and animals that make the water look dirty.

Then... disaster! When floods hit, some of the carp escaped into nearby streams that flow into the Mississippi River. The carp began to spread through the Mississippi and its smaller branches, or tributaries.

> Fishermen are often amazed at the size of the Asian carp they pull in. There are no freshwater fish in North America big enough to eat an adult Asian carp.

Many people, including scientists and fishermen, are concerned about the growth of the carp population. For one thing, the carp are unusually big and strong. They grow as long as five feet and can weigh more than 100 pounds.

They can leap ten feet out of the water, which makes them dangerous because they can strike and injure boaters. But that is not the main threat posed by Asian carp.

TAKING OVER

Surprisingly, Asian carp don't eat other fish. Instead, they eat tiny animals and little plants called algae. Because they are so large, they have huge appetites. They eat the food that other fish and water creatures depend on to live. Then there's not enough food for the other fish, whose populations decrease.

The fish that are left have to compete against an ever-growing population of Asian carp, which can produce hundreds of thousands of eggs at a time. This means that the carp population can grow incredibly fast. Also, young carp grow quickly and soon become so big that no other fish prey on them.

OTHER INVADERS

Dozens of other harmful species have already invaded the Great Lakes. Read the photo captions to learn about a few of these species.

∨ Sea lampreys are the vampires of the Great Lakes. They have long bodies like eels. Their mouths are like suction cups. They attach themselves to fish and suck their blood. The victims often die. In this photo, sea lampreys attach to a brown trout.

With such fast rates of growth, the longer the Asian carp live in an area, the more they take over. They crowd out other fish.

Asian carp have now taken over much of the Mississippi River system, from Minnesota in the north to Louisiana in the south. In Illinois, they've spread to within a few miles of Lake Michigan. Experts fear that if they get into the Great Lakes, they could cause even more harm than zebra mussels and sea lampreys. For example, Asian carp could wipe out many native fish species. This could cause the fishing industry to collapse. Carp could also greatly harm the Great Lakes ecosystems by reducing the number of different fish found there.

∧ The tiny shellfish called zebra mussels cluster in huge colonies. They block water pipes at power plants and water treatment facilities. They damage boats, piers, and buoys.

∧ Purple loosestrife can grow up to seven feet tall. It can produce several million seeds a year. This plant spreads and crowds out native plant along the marshy shores of the Great Lakes.

ALIEN SPECIES: KEEP OUT!

The Asian carp invasion is a complicated problem. So far there are a few possible solutions, but none of them is perfect.

In northeastern Illinois, near the southern tip of Lake Michigan, a network of **canals** links the Mississippi River system to the Great Lakes. A canal is a human-made waterway. For Asian carp, the canals represent the easiest path to the lakes.

One way engineers are trying to stop the carp is by putting electrical barriers into the canals. When fish approach the electrical barriers, they feel a shock and swim the other way. But if the carp get through the barriers somehow, they could spread quickly. Is this the best solution to this alien problem? Read more about the solutions and decide for yourself.

∨ Army engineers have put up electrical barriers underwater in these canals to keep Asian carp out. However, these barriers can also be dangerous to people.

Danger
Entering Electric Fish Barriers
High Risk of Electric Shock
No Swimming, Diving, Fishing, or Mooring

SOLUTION 1:

Installing electric barriers 50 miles from Lake Michigan seems to be keeping Asian carp out of the Great Lakes pretty well so far. Only a few carp have been found between the barriers and Lake Michigan, and they were removed. The downside to this solution is that the electric barriers are expensive, and if they ever lose their electric current, the Asian carp will be able to swim right into the lakes.

SOLUTION 2:

Some people say the only way to keep the carp out of the Great Lakes is to close off the canals from the Mississippi River system. Closing the canals might stop Asian carp from entering the Great Lakes, but it would also prevent ships from using the canals to move from the Great Lakes into other bodies of water such as the Atlantic Ocean. That would make it very difficult to move ships full of goods throughout the country.

WHAT DO YOU THINK?

Many people are concerned about the spread of the Asian carp into the Great Lakes. Are electric barriers the answer? If not, can we find another solution—such as closing off the canals—and act on it in time?

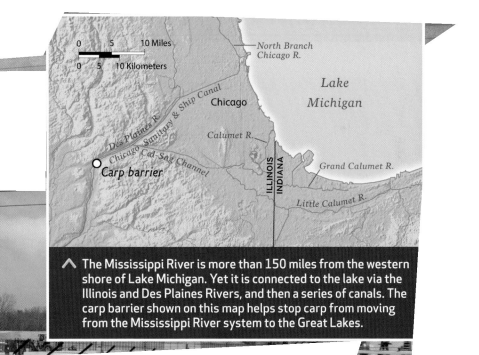

The Mississippi River is more than 150 miles from the western shore of Lake Michigan. Yet it is connected to the lake via the Illinois and Des Plaines Rivers, and then a series of canals. The carp barrier shown on this map helps stop carp from moving from the Mississippi River system to the Great Lakes.

Check In What could happen if Asian carp get into the Great Lakes?

Chicago's Air and Water Show

by Bryon Cahill

VROOM! **A thundering roar fills the air above your head. High in the sky above Lake Michigan, six mighty jets swoop down. White smoke trails behind. Then, at a sharp angle, the jets shoot up. They twist and turn as they cut through the air.**

The whole time, the jets remain in a diamond-shape formation. They fly mere feet from one another, sometimes with as little as 18 inches separating them.

Each year, Chicago's Air and Water Show attracts more than 1.5 million people to the area. It encourages **tourism**, which is good for Chicago businesses. Chicago welcomes the crowds who enjoy the city and spend their money here. Restaurants

Pilots practice their stunts before the show in the air above Chicago's lakefront.

and hotels are packed, and Chicago's stores are filled with shoppers. The tourism the Air and Water Show brings to the city provides jobs and dollars to Chicago, which helps the city's **economy**, or the money and goods that come into and go out of a community, nation, or business.

Why is Chicago's Lake Michigan shore such a perfect setting for the oldest free air and water show in the United States? The lake waters stretch east, so planes have a large, safe flying area for their performance. And Chicago's many beaches, parks, and harbors extend far enough to the north and south to allow all of the spectators to find places to watch from blankets, beach chairs, and benches. Some people even board cruise ships to see the show from the water.

The Show Takes Off

How did it all begin? The festivities started in 1959 as a small celebration for children in a Chicago Park District day camp. With a total budget of only $88, the event included activities such as water ballet, water skiers, and a diving contest. The Coast Guard also hosted a demonstration to show how to use a helicopter to rescue someone from the lake.

Crowds can view impressive sights in both the water and the sky.

The Air and Water Show has become bigger every year since. In 1960, the U.S. Army Air Force Thunderbirds performed for the first time, zooming around in a dizzying performance of fancy rolls, dives, and passes. Also for the first time, the U.S. Army Golden Knights Parachute Team jumped into the skies over Chicago that year, plunging down to land in the waters of Lake Michigan.

Today's Air and Water Show spectators still expect to be entertained by such sights. In one breathtaking act, a helicopter rolls and flips through the air, even turning upside down. Its daredevil pilot is one of only three helicopter pilots in the world with a license to perform such dangerous stunts.

The audience keeps cool in Lake Michigan while watching daredevil pilots perform amazing stunts.

A member of the U.S. Navy Parachute Team lands in front of a packed crowd. The team is known as the "Leap Frogs."

The Wild Blue Yonder

Some performers are so popular that they return each year. The current Air and Water Show still features parachute jumpers. They jump from 12,500 feet in the air—more than two miles high! As many as 14 jumpers work together to make patterns as they fall. And, out on the water, the modern Coast Guard still gives a search-and-rescue demonstration.

Some years, the U.S. Army Air Force Thunderbirds are the headliners of the show. Other years, the U.S. Navy Blue Angels are the main attraction. How fast do the Blue Angels go? Hold on to your hats because the fastest plane they fly—the F/A-18 Hornet aircraft—can reach speeds of up to 1,400 miles per hour (mph). That is twice the speed of sound! 1,400 mph is too fast for a jet at a spectator show to go, though. The pilots are only allowed to fly at top speeds of about 700 mph. That's still more than ten times as fast as the average highway speed limit.

The Blue Angels' jets all carry the U.S. Navy's official colors—blue and gold.

The skill required to fly these planes takes years of training. The pilots of the Blue Angels need at least 1,200 hours of flying these jets to make the team. The commanding officer of the Blue Angels needs at least 3,000 hours of training. The pilots love showing off their skills to the people who come to the Air and Water Show. And every August, audiences pour into the city of Chicago to see what amazing feats these pilots can achieve.

∨ The Blue Angels perform at many air shows. About 11 million people see them each year.

Check In How does the presence of the Air and Water Show affect the economy of Chicago?

THE WRECK OF THE MIGHTY FITZ

by Chris Siegel and
Stephanie Herbek

The Great Lakes are some of the most dangerous waters on Earth. It can be extremely difficult to **navigate**, or find one's way through, the Great Lakes. They are known for sudden, violent storms and huge, crashing waves. These waves can—and quite possibly, did—force a ship down to the cold, dark depths of the lake with little warning.

The S.S. *Edmund Fitzgerald*, or *Mighty Fitz*, was the largest carrier ship on the Great Lakes when it launched in 1958. Weighing 13,632 tons and stretching 729 feet long, it had carried more than a million tons of iron ore during its long life. But on November 9, 1975, after years of toting cargo across the Great Lakes, the *Mighty Fitz* left Superior, Wisconsin, on what would be its final voyage. Captain Ernest M. McSorley was at the helm.

Traveling a common route across Lake Superior, the *Mighty Fitz* met up with another carrier ship, the S.S. *Arthur M. Anderson*. Both ships were headed for the Great Lakes steel mills. On November 10, 1975—the second day of their voyage—a massive winter storm blew in. It slammed the boats with hurricane-force winds and waves up to 35 feet high. The *Mighty Fitz* disappeared into the depths of Lake Superior. It carried 29 crew members down with it.

< This painting depicts the final voyage of the S.S. *Edmund Fitzgerald*. "S.S." stands for *steamship* in a ship's name.

EDMUND FITZGERALD

NO CALL FOR HELP?

The *Anderson* and *Fitzgerald* had maintained radio contact throughout their voyage. Around 7:10 p.m. on November 10, a crewman on the *Anderson* radioed to see how the *Mighty Fitz* was handling the storm. He received a brief response: "We are holding our own." Shortly after this transmission, the *Fitzgerald* disappeared from the *Anderson's* radar screen. It was never seen above water again. The following is a transcript of the actual radio transmission that took place between the crews on that fateful night.

Fitzgerald: Anderson, this is the Fitzgerald. I have sustained some topside damage. I have a fence rail laid down, two vents lost or damaged, and a **list**. I'm *checking down*. Will you stay by me 'til I get to Whitefish?

> **slowing the ship's speed**

> **tilt to one side**

Anderson: "Charlie" on that, Fitzgerald.

> **got it**

# # #

Anderson: Fitzgerald, this is Anderson. Have you checked down?

Fitzgerald: Yes, we have.

Anderson: Fitzgerald, we are about 10 miles behind you, and gaining about one and a half miles per hour. Fitzgerald, there is a target 19 miles ahead of us. So the target would be nine miles on ahead of you.

> **another ship**

Fitzgerald: Well, am I going to clear?

Anderson: Yes, he is going to pass to the west of you.

Fitzgerald: Well, fine.

Anderson: By the way, Fitzgerald, how are you making out with your problems?

Fitzgerald: We are holding our own.

> **doing OK**

Anderson: Okay, fine. I'll be talking to you later.

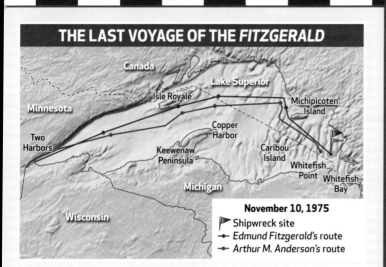

November 10, 1975

⚑ Shipwreck site
•→ *Edmund Fitzgerald's* route
•→ *Arthur M. Anderson's* route

WHAT HAPPENED TO THE *MIGHTY FITZ*?

No **distress call**, or call for help, ever came from the *Fitzgerald* on that stormy night. This has baffled investigators for decades. The ship and its crew simply disappeared into the cold, green waters of Lake Superior. Did the storm sink the *Mighty Fitz*?

The Great Lakes can be more risky for ships and sailors than the ocean. Hurricane-force storms blow in with virtually no warning, especially in November, a particularly dangerous month in this region. Moving goods across the Great Lakes is a risky business for ships, and the *Mighty Fitz* was no exception.

Many have speculated on the cause of the shipwreck. Some believe the *Fitzgerald* may have fallen victim to the high waves of the storm. Others believe the ship might have hit the bottom of the lake and broken apart. The sinking remains a mystery.

THREE SINKING THEORIES

⋀ Both ends of the ship may have been pushed up by waves. The *Fitzgerald's* heavy cargo was located in the center of the ship. This could have caused the ship to crack in half.

⋀ "Three Sisters" are a series of three gigantic waves. They may have struck the *Fitzgerald*, flooding and sinking it.

⋀ The *Fitzgerald* passed a shallow area near Caribou Island. If the ship got too close, it may have "bottomed out," or hit the bottom of the lake in a shallow area, cracking on impact.

> ⌃ A diver inspects the wreckage of the *Edmund Fitzgerald*, more than 500 feet underwater.

REMEMBERING THE *MIGHTY FITZ*

Shortly after radio contact was lost with the *Fitzgerald*, the concerned crew of the *Anderson* discovered two lifeboats and other **debris** floating in the water, but no sign of survivors. Later, the Coast Guard used planes, ships, and **sonar** to locate two large pieces of debris in the area of the shipwreck. They had found the *Mighty Fitz*.

Thousands of shipwrecks lie on the bottom of the Great Lakes. The wreckage of the *Fitzgerald* includes intact front and back ends and a broken midsection. It lies deep in Lake Superior in Canadian territory. Few divers have seen it, but every year, better diving technology makes it possible for more to visit. Out of respect for the sailors lost in the wreck, the Canadian government has limited access to the wreckage.

On July 4, 1995, the 200-pound bronze bell was removed from the *Fitzgerald's* wreckage by the Great Lakes Shipwreck Historical Society. It was a joint effort between the National Geographic Society, Canadian Navy, Sony Corporation, and a Michigan tribe of Chippewa Indians. The

∧ The ship's bell had water damage when it was raised from the wreckage. It was restored before being placed in the museum.

bell is now on display in the Great Lakes Shipwreck Museum in Paradise, Michigan, as a memorial to the lost crew. It is rung 29 times—once for each lost crew member—at a memorial held on the anniversary of the shipwreck every year.

Check In   What sequence of events led to the sinking of the *Fitzgerald?*

Discuss

1. What connections can you make among the five selections in this book? How do you think the selections are related?

2. Would you like to live in a region that had lake-effect weather? Why or why not?

3. What are some of the effects of invasive species on the Great Lakes?

4. Consider the three different theories that try to explain why the *Fitzgerald* sank. Which one do you believe is the best explanation for what happened? Why?

5. What do you still wonder about the Great Lakes and the issues that affect the region?